# Watson

by Iain Gray

PUBLISHING

WRITING *to* REMEMBER

79 Main Street, Newtongrange,
Midlothian EH22 4NA
Tel: 0131 344 0414
E-mail: info@lang-syne.co.uk
www.langsyneshop.co.uk

Design by Dorothy Meikle
Printed by Printwell Ltd
© Lang Syne Publishers Ltd 2023

All rights reserved. No part of this publication may be reproduced, stored or introduced into a retrieval system, or transmitted in any form or by any means (electronic, mechanical, photocopying, recording or otherwise) without the prior written permission of Lang Syne Publishers Ltd.

ISBN 978-1-85217-602-0

# Watson

**MOTTO:**
Fidelity is my glory.

**CREST:**
The head of a griffin
(and)
a falcon
(and)
a stoat.

**NAME** variations include:
Walterson
Watt
Watts
Wattson
MacWattie *(Gaelic)*

*Chapter one:*

# The origins of popular surnames

by George Forbes and Iain Gray

***If you don't know where you came from, you won't know where you're going** is a frequently quoted observation and one that has a particular resonance today when there has been a marked upsurge in interest in genealogy, with increasing numbers of people curious to trace their family roots.*

Main sources for genealogical research include census returns and official records of births, marriages and deaths – and the key to unlocking the detail they contain is obviously a family surname, one that has been 'inherited' and passed from generation to generation.

No matter our station in life, we all have a surname – but it was not until about the middle of the fourteenth century that the practice of being identified by a particular surname became commonly established throughout the British Isles.

Previous to this, it was normal for a person to be identified through the use of only a forename.

But as population gradually increased and there were many more people with the same forename, surnames were adopted to distinguish one person, or community, from another.

Many common English surnames are patronymic in origin, meaning they stem from the forename of one's father – with 'Johnson,' for example, indicating 'son of John.'

It was the Normans, in the wake of their eleventh century conquest of Anglo-Saxon England, a pivotal moment in the nation's history, who first brought surnames into usage – although it was a gradual process.

For the Normans, these were names initially based on the title of their estates, local villages and chateaux in France to distinguish and identify these landholdings.

Such grand descriptions also helped enhance the prestige of these warlords and generally glorify their lofty positions high above the humble serfs slaving away below in the pecking order who had only single names, often with Biblical connotations as in Pierre and Jacques.

The only descriptive distinctions among the peasantry concerned their occupations, like 'Pierre the swineherd' or 'Jacques the ferryman.'

Roots of surnames that came into usage in England not only included Norman-French, but also Old French, Old Norse, Old English, Middle English, German, Latin, Greek, Hebrew and the Gaelic languages of the Celts.

The Normans themselves were originally Vikings, or 'Northmen', who raided, colonised and eventually settled down around the French coastline.

They had sailed up the Seine in their long-boats in 900AD under their ferocious leader Rollo and ruled the roost in north eastern France before sailing over to conquer England in 1066 under Duke William of Normandy – better known to posterity as William the Conqueror, or King William I of England.

Granted lands in the newly-conquered England, some of their descendants later acquired territories in Wales, Scotland and Ireland – taking not only their own surnames, but also the practice of adopting a surname, with them.

But it was in England where Norman rule and custom first impacted, particularly in relation to the adoption of surnames.

This is reflected in the famous *Domesday Book*, a massive survey of much of England and Wales, ordered by William I, to determine who owned what, what it was worth and therefore how much they were liable to pay in taxes to the voracious Royal Exchequer.

Completed in 1086 and now held in the National Archives in Kew, London, 'Domesday' was an Old English word meaning 'Day of Judgement.'

This was because, in the words of one contemporary chronicler, "its decisions, like those of the Last Judgement, are unalterable."

It had been a requirement of all those English landholders – from the richest to the poorest – that they identify themselves for the purposes of the survey and for future reference by means of a surname.

This is why the *Domesday Book*, although written in Latin as was the practice for several centuries with both civic and ecclesiastical records, is an invaluable source for the early appearance of a wide range of English surnames.

Several of these names were coined in connection with occupations.

These include Baker and Smith, while Cooks, Chamberlains, Constables and Porters were to be found carrying out duties in large medieval households.

The church's influence can be found in names such as Bishop, Friar and Monk while the popular name of Bennett derives from the late fifth to mid-sixth century Saint Benedict, founder of the Benedictine order of monks.

The early medical profession is represented by Barber, while businessmen produced names that include Merchant and Sellers.

Down at the village watermill, the names that cropped up included Millar/Miller, Walker and Fuller, while other self-explanatory trades included Cooper, Tailor, Mason and Wright.

Even the scenery was utilised as in Moor, Hill, Wood and Forrest – while the hunt and the chase supplied names that include Hunter, Falconer, Fowler and Fox.

Colours are also a source of popular surnames, as in Black, Brown, Gray/Grey, Green and White, and would have denoted the colour of the clothing the person habitually wore or, apart from the obvious exception of 'Green', one's hair colouring or even complexion.

The surname Red developed into Reid, while

Blue was rare and no-one wanted to be associated with yellow.

Rather self-important individuals took surnames that include Goodman and Wiseman, while physical attributes crept into surnames such as Small and Little.

Many families proudly boast the heraldic device known as a Coat of Arms, as featured on our front cover.

The central motif of the Coat of Arms would originally have been what was borne on the shield of a warrior to distinguish himself from others on the battlefield.

Not featured on the Coat of Arms, but highlighted on page three, is the family motto and related crest – with the latter frequently different from the central motif.

Adding further variety to the rich cultural heritage that is represented by surnames is the appearance in recent times in lists of the 100 most common names found in England of ones that include Khan, Patel and Singh – names that have proud roots in the vast sub-continent of India.

Echoes of a far distant past can still be found in our surnames and they can be borne with pride in commemoration of our forebears.

*Chapter two:*

# Ancient origins

**A name of truly martial roots, 'Watson' – meaning 'son of Wat', or 'son of Watt' – is a diminutive of the forename 'Walter' and derives from the Germanic 'wald', meaning 'rule' and 'heri', indicating 'army.'**

The ancestors of those who would come to bear it as a surname in the wake of the Norman Conquest of 1066 were present on British shores from much earlier times.

This means that flowing through the veins of many English bearers of the name today may well be the blood of those Germanic tribes who invaded and settled in the south and east of the island of Britain from about the early fifth century.

Known as the Anglo-Saxons, they were composed of the Jutes, from the area of the Jutland Peninsula in modern Denmark, the Saxons from Lower Saxony, in modern Germany and the Angles from the Angeln area of Germany.

It was the Angles who gave the name 'Engla land', or 'Aengla land' – better known as 'England.'

They held sway in what became England from approximately 550 until the Norman Conquest, with the main kingdoms those of Sussex, Wessex, Northumbria, Mercia, Kent, East Anglia and Essex.

Whoever controlled the most powerful of these kingdoms was tacitly recognised as overall 'king' – one of the most noted being Alfred the Great, King of Wessex from 871 to 899.

It was during his reign that the famous *Anglo-Saxon Chronicle* was compiled – an invaluable source of Anglo-Saxon history – while Alfred was designated in early documents as *Rex Anglorum Saxonum*, King of the English Saxons. Other important Anglo-Saxon works include the epic *Beowulf* and the seventh century *Caedmon's Hymn*.

Through the Anglo-Saxons, the language known as Old English developed, later transforming from the eleventh century into Middle English.

It was following the Norman Conquest that, within an astonishingly short space of time, Norman manners, customs and law were imposed on England – laying the basis for what subsequently became established 'English' custom and practice.

But beneath the surface, old Anglo-Saxon culture was not totally eradicated, with some aspects absorbed into those of the Normans, while faint echoes of the Anglo-Saxon past is still seen today in the form of popular surnames such as Watson.

A name that features prominently in the frequently turbulent historical record, it is particularly identified with modern-day County Rutland – an area of central England that is bounded in the southeast by Northamptonshire, west and north by Leicestershire and northeast by Lincolnshire – and where a family of the name held the seat of Rockingham Castle.

Born in 1584, the son of Sir Edward Watson and Anne Digby, a daughter of Kenelm Digby of Stoke Dry, Rutland, Lewis Watson, 1st Baron Rockingham, was a prominent Royalist during the bitter and bloody mid-seventeenth century English Civil War.

The monarch Charles I had incurred the wrath of Parliament by his insistence on the 'divine right' of monarchs, and added to this was Parliament's fear of Catholic 'subversion' against the state and the king's stubborn refusal to grant demands for religious and constitutional concessions.

Matters came to a head with the outbreak of the civil war in 1642, with Parliamentary forces, known as the New Model Army and commanded by

Oliver Cromwell and Sir Thomas Fairfax, arrayed against the Royalist army of the king.

In what became an increasingly bloody and complex conflict, spreading to Scotland and Ireland and with rapidly shifting loyalties on both sides, the king was eventually captured and executed in January of 1649 on the orders of Parliament.

Lewis Watson, meanwhile, who had been knighted in 1608, was elected Member of Parliament (MP) for Lincoln in 1621 and served as Sheriff of Northamptonshire from 1632 to 1633.

It was for his services to the ill-fated Charles I that in the early stages of the civil war and eight years before his death in 1653 that he was created 1st Baron Rockingham.

His grandson, also named Lewis Watson, the eldest son of Edward Watson, 2nd Baron Rockingham and Lady Anne Wentworth, daughter of Thomas Wentworth, 1st Earl of Stafford, was the Whig politician who served for a time as MP for Canterbury.

Having held posts that included Lord Lieutenant of Kent and, from 1705 to 1708 Master of the Cinque Ports, he was created 1st Earl of Rockingham shortly before his death in 1724.

Not related to the Rutland family of Watsons,

but also the recipient of high honours and distinction, Sir Brooke Watson, 1st Baronet of the name, has a particularly unusual claim to fame.

This is through a painting that he especially commissioned known as *Watson and the Shark*.

Born in 1735 in Plymouth, Devon, he was orphaned when aged six and sent to live with an uncle and aunt in Boston, Massachusetts.

His uncle, a merchant who had trade links with the West Indies, signed his nephew up to serve as a crew member on one of his trading vessels after the young lad had expressed an interest in a life at sea.

In 1749, while swimming alone in Havana harbour, Cuba, the 14-year-old Watson was attacked by a shark which, before he could be rescued, removed the flesh from below the calf of his right leg and the bottom of his right foot at the ankle.

His leg had to be amputated below the knee but, undeterred, Watson went on to serve in other merchant vessels after his uncle's business entered into bankruptcy.

Serving on vessels that took provisions to a British Army base at Fort Lawrence, Nova Scotia, he came to the attention of the authorities and was appointed as a commissary.

Known as "the wooden-legged commissary", he returned to Britain in 1759 and set up his own highly-successful business with trade links to Boston, Montreal and other far-flung places.

Serving as MP for the City of London from 1784 until 1793 and as Lord Mayor of London in 1796, it had been in 1774 that he commissioned the celebrated artist John Singleton Copley to paint *Watson and the Shark*, depicting him in the shark attack as a youth that had resulted in the loss of his right leg below the knee.

Completed in 1778, the painting was exhibited at the Royal Academy in that year while, in 1963, it was bought from Christ's Hospital, London, by the National Gallery of Art in Washington, D.C.; created a baronet, Watson died in 1807.

While the artist John Singleton Copley gained fame through his *Watson and the Shark* painting, George Watson was the celebrated Scottish portrait painter who in 1820 was appointed first president of the prestigious Royal Scottish Academy.

Born in 1767 in Overmains, Berwickshire, he died in 1837 while his son William Smellie Watson, born in 1796 and who died in 1874, was also a noted portrait artist.

*Chapter three:*

# Creative minds

**Bearers of the Watson name have stamped an indelible mark on the worlds of invention, medicine and the sciences.**

Born in Edinburgh in 1908, George Whyte-Watson was the surgeon who, appointed as consultant to St Luke's Hospital and Bradford Royal Infirmary in 1946, along with his colleague the pathologist Professor Robert Lowry Turner carried out pioneering work into the treatment of breast cancer by the use of chemotherapy.

Also responsible for stressing the importance of 'self-examination' as part of the procedure for detecting breast cancer, he died in 1974 – while there is a memorial plaque to Watson and Professor Turner in Bradford Cathedral.

Born in Chicago in 1928, James Dewey Watson is the American geneticist, biologist and zoologist best known as the discoverer, along with Francis Crick, of the structure of the 'building block' of life known as DNA.

It was while working with Crick at Cambridge

University's Cavendish Laboratory in 1953 that he discovered the DNA 'double helix' structure.

In 1962, he, Crick and Maurice Wilkins were awarded the Nobel Prize in Physiology or Medicine "for their discoveries concerning the molecular structure of nucleic acids and its significance for information transfer in living material."

Watson, whose maternal grandfather was a tailor from Glasgow, Scotland, and maternal grandmother of Irish roots, is the recipient of honours that include the Benjamin Franklin Medal for Distinguished Achievement and the author of best-selling books that include his 1968 *The Double Helix*.

Noted as having his surname as one of the first words spoken on the telephone, Thomas Watson was the assistant to Alexander Graham Bell, the inventor of that indispensable device.

Born in 1854 in Salem, Massachusetts, he had been hired by Bell while he worked on the invention at Boston University.

It had been in 1876, with Bell and Watson in adjoining rooms equipped with a rudimentary telephone device, that Watson heard Bell's words: "Mr Watson, come here, I want you."

Watson, who died in 1934, used money from his royalties for his participation in the invention to found the Fore River Ship and Engine Building Company, which became one of the largest shipyards in the United States and was eventually taken over by Bethlehem Steel.

Recognised as having played a vital role during the Battle of Britain that was fought over the skies of southern and eastern England in the summer of 1940, Sir Robert Watson-Watt was the Scottish pioneer in the development of radar born in 1892 in Brechin, Angus.

A descendant of James Watt, the engineer and inventor of the first practical steam engine, he began work on what became radar – derived from Radio Detection and Ranging – in 1936 when employed by the British Air Ministry at its Bawdsey Research Station near Felixstowe, Suffolk.

Radar, which emits radio pulses that are 'reflected' back from a target such as an aircraft, allowed for the early detection of incoming swarms of German Luftwaffe bombers and fighters – in turn enabling the 'scrambling' of fighter planes to meet and deal with the threat.

Knighted and awarded £50,000 by a grateful

British government , it was after the war, while driving in Canada, that he was pulled over by a traffic policeman whose radar-equipped 'gun' had detected him exceeding the speed limit.

Watson-Watt is said to have responded: "Had I known what you were going to do with it, I would never have invented it!" He died in 1973.

Born in 1910 in the coal mining community of Mexborough, Yorkshire, the son of a school headmaster, Donald Watson was the animal rights activist who coined the term 'vegan' and founded the Vegan Society.

Shunning all animal foodstuffs and other animal products, it was in Leicester in 1944 that, along with his wife Dorothy and other like-minded friends, he founded the Vegan Society – suggesting the term 'vegan' as "the beginning and end of 'vegetarian', because veganism starts with vegetarianism and carries it through to its logical conclusion."

He died, aged 95, in 2005.

In the world of politics, Dr Bruce Watson, born in 1910 in Rubislaw, Aberdeen was the professor of organic chemistry who was leader of the Scottish National Party (SNP) from 1945 to 1947; he died in 1988.

Born in 1949 in Cambuslang, South Lanarkshire, but raised in Invergowrie, Perth and Kinross, Michael Goodall Watson is the Scottish Labour Party politician better known as Mike Watson and more formally as Baron Watson of Invergowrie.

Elected to Parliament as MP for the former Glasgow Central constituency in 1989 he served until the seat was abolished in 1997, and he was created a life peer.

Elected as a Member of the Scottish Parliament (MSP) for the Glasgow Cathcart constituency in both 1999 and 2003, it was while serving as an MSP that he introduced the Private Member's Bill, the controversial Protection of Wild Mammals Bill to outlaw fox hunting – which received Royal Assent in 2002 as the Protection of Wild Mammals (Scotland) Act.

Serving on the Scottish Executive from 2001 to 2003 as Minister for Tourism Culture and Sport, it was in November of 2004 that the gifted politician fell from grace after being found guilty of a charge of wilful fire-raising.

The incident had occurred in an Edinburgh hotel following the Scottish Politician of the Year Awards.

Having already resigned from the Scottish Parliament and also as a director of Dundee United Football Club, he was sentenced to 16 months imprisonment, the judge informing him that consumption of alcohol "neither excuses nor fully explains your behaviour."

After having served eight months of his sentence, under current rules that make it impossible for a peer to 'resign' from the House of Lords, he is still entitled to sit in the House.

Also in the world of politics, Tom Watson is the Labour Party politician who, as a member of the government's Culture, Media and Sports Committee was closely involved in questioning people who appeared before a special inquiry into the News International 'phone-hacking scandal'.

Born in 1967, he has served as MP for West Bromwich East since 2001, while in 2011 he was appointed Deputy Chair of the Labour Party.

Along with the journalist Martin Hickman, he is also the author of the 2012 *Dial M for Murdoch*.

*Chapter four:*

# On the world stage

**A star, along with Daniel Radcliffe and Rupert Grint of all eight of the *Harry Potter* series of films, Emma Watson is the English actress and model born Emma Charlotte Duerre Watson in Paris in 1990.**

The daughter of British lawyers who had been working in Paris, she was aged five when she returned to Britain and, a year later, began studying acting, singing and dancing at a theatre school.

Although she appeared in a number of small theatre and school productions, she had never acted professionally until cast, aged nine, for the role of Hermione Granger in *Harry Potter and the Philosopher's Stone*, the first in the highly successful *Harry Potter* series based on the best-selling novels by J.K. Rowling.

Named in 2010 as one of Hollywood's highest paid female stars and estimated to have earned more than £10m from her involvement in the *Harry Potter* series, she made her modelling debut, for a British clothing range, in 2009 – while in 2013 in a worldwide poll conducted by *Empire* magazine she was voted "Sexiest Female Movie Star."

Other screen credits include the 2012 *The Perks of Being a Wallflower*, the 2013 *The Bling Ring* and the 2014 *Noah*, while she also starred in *The Tale of Despereaux*, and a 2007 television adaptation of the Noel Streatfeild novel *Ballet Shoes*.

Born in 1967 in Islington, London, **Emily Watson** is the award-winning actress who began her career on the stage and who has worked with the Royal Shakespeare Company.

Nominated for the Olivier Award for Best Actress for a 2013 production of *Uncle Vanya*, she is the recipient of Academy Award nominations for her roles in the 1996 film *Breaking the Waves* and the 1998 *Hilary and Jackie*.

With other major film credits that include the 1999 *Angela's Ashes*, the 2001 *Gosford Park* and, from 2013, *The Book Thief*, her television credits include the 2011 drama *Appropriate Adult*, for which she won a BAFTA Award for Best Actress.

With the rather unusual claim to big screen fame of having portrayed Adolf Hitler in no fewer than nine films, **Bobby Watson** was the American actor born Robert Watson Knucher in Springfield, Illinois, in 1888.

Beginning his career in silent films, he later appeared as Hitler in the 1942 *The Devil with Hitler*, reprising the role in other films that include the 1944 *The Hitler Gang*, the 1961 *On the Double* and, three years before his death in 1965, *Four Horsemen of the Apocalypse*.

Born Deborah Lynn Watson in Culver City, Los Angeles, in 1949, **Debbie Watson** is the American retired actress whose film roles include that of Marilyn Munster in the 1966 *Munster, Go Home!*

Other film credits include, co-starring with Roddy McDowall, the 1967 *The Cool Ones*, while before her retirement from acting in 1971 she also appeared on television in *Love, American Style*.

Also now retired from the film world, **David Watson**, born in 1940 in Austin, Texas, to British parents, appeared in a range of television series that include *Rawhide*, *The Girl from U.N.C.L.E.*, *Daniel Boone* and *The Bionic Woman*, while his big screen credits include the 1970 *Beneath the Planet of the Apes* and, from 2002, *The Wannabees*.

A veteran actor of the stage, television and the big screen, **Tom Watson** was the Scottish actor born in 1932 in Auchinleck, East Ayrshire.

His many television credits include *Dixon of*

*Dock Green*, *Dr Finlay's Casebook*, *Inspector Rebus*, *Your Cheatin' Heart* and *The Big Man*, while film credits include the 1990 *The Silent Scream*; with stage credits that include the 1990 production *The Ship*, he died in 2001.

Born in 1915 in Thorney, Cambridgeshire, **Jack Watson** was the English actor who, in addition to an early role in the television soap *Coronation Street* as the character Elsie Tanner's lover, also appeared in television series and dramas that include *Edge of Darkness*.

With film credits that include the 1963 *This Sporting Life*, the 1967 *Tobruk* and the 1978 *The Wild Geese*, he died in 1999.

An actor of the stage, television and film and also a producer, **James Watson**, also known as Jimmy Watson, was born in Glasgow in 1970.

It was after training at the Drama Studio, London and the Focus Theatre Studio, Dublin, that he began his acting career with the role of Dr John McEwan in the Irish television soap *Fair City*.

Co-founder of Celtic Mouse Productions (Ireland), other television credits include the Scottish soap *River City* and the 2000 American mini-series Frank Herbert's *Dune*.

Best known for her title role in the television series *La Femme Nikita*, Faith Susan Alberta Watson, born in Toronto in 1955, is the Canadian actress better known as **Alberta Watson**.

With other television credits that include the drama series *Heartland*, for which she won a 2011 Gemini Award, she has also starred in films that include the 1996 *Shoemaker*, for which she received a Genie Award nomination for Best Actress and, from 1997, *The Sweet Hereafter*.

Born in 1928 in Sunningdale, Berkshire, **Moray Watson** is the English stage, television and film actor whose many television credits include *Compact*, *Rumpole of the Bailey*, *The Pallisers*, the 1980 series *Pride and Prejudice* and the 1991 to 1993 *The Larkins*.

Big screen credits include the 1953 *The Quatermass Experiment* and, playing opposite Cary Grant and Robert Mitchum, the 1960 *The Grass is Greener*.

Bearers of the Watson name have also excelled in the highly competitive world of sport and no-one less so than the famed American golfer **Tom Watson**.

Born Thomas Sturges Watson in Kansas

City, Missouri, in 1949 and introduced to the game as a young boy by his father, he has won to date eight major championships that include five Open Championships, one U.S. Open and two Masters titles.

Now playing mainly on the Champions Tour after having played on the Professional Golfers Association (PGA) Tour and recognised as one of the greatest links players of all time, he has played in five Ryder Cup teams, including as captain of the American team at the 2014 Ryder Cup.

Also on the golf course, Gerry Lester Watson, Jr., better known as **Bubba Watson** and who was born in 1978 in Bagdad, Florida, is the American PGA Tour player whose many wins include the Masters Tournament in both 2012 and 2014.

On the tennis court, **Heather Watson**, born in 1992 in Guernsey, is the player who in 2012 gained the ranking of British female No. 1. Taking up the tennis racquet when aged seven, she won the British Under-14 Championship in 2006 and the Japan Open in 2012.

In the high-speed sport of motor racing, **John Watson,** born in Northern Ireland in 1949, is the former driver whose wins include the 1981 British

Grand Prix; the recipient of an MBE, he is now a commentator for SkySports.

Born in Aberdeen in 1913 and emigrating from Scotland to Canada as a youth, Robert B. Watson was the jockey better known as **Bobby Watson**.

In a horse racing career that spanned more than 25 years, he won nine of the Classic races that now form the Canadian Triple Crown series and was a three-time winner of the Canadian Championship; an inductee of the Canadian Horse Racing Hall of Fame, he died in 1979.

Taking to the water, **Jessica Watson**, born on the Gold Coast, Queensland, in 1993, is the Australian sailor who became, unofficially, the youngest person to sail non-stop and unassisted around the world.

This was when, aged only 16, she left Sydney on October 18, 2009, heading over the Pacific, Atlantic and Indian oceans, returning to Sydney three days before her seventeenth birthday on May 15, 2010.

Her feat, however, did not meet with the World Sailing Speed Record Council's strict criteria for circumnavigation of the globe.

Nevertheless, she was named the 2011 Young

Australian of the Year and, a year later, awarded a Medal of the Order of Australia.

From sport to the creative art of photography, **Albert Watson** is the Scottish photographer famed for his art, celebrity and fashion work – despite the disability of being blind in one eye since birth.

Born in Edinburgh in 1942 but growing up in Penicuik, Midlothian, and named by *Photo District News* magazine as one of the 20 most influential photographers of all time, he studied at Duncan of Jordanstone College of Art, Dundee, and the Royal College of Art, London.

Immigrating to the Unites States with his wife, Elizabeth, in the early 1970s, his first major assignment as a photographer was for the beauty products manufacturer Max Factor, followed by work for fashion magazines that include *Vogue*, *GQ* and *Mademoiselle*.

One of his most famous images, which graced the front cover of the 1973 Christmas issue of *Harper's Bazaar* magazine, was a portrait of film director Alfred Hitchcock holding a dead goose with a ribbon around its neck.

Other famous figures he has captured on camera include the Queen and former U.S. President

Bill Clinton, while he has shot more than 40 covers for *Rolling Stone* music magazine.

Winner of a Grammy Award in 1975 for his photography for the Mason Proffit album *Come and Gone*, he has also photographed for film posters that include the 2003 *Kill Bill*, the 2005 *Memoirs of a Geisha* and the 2006 *The Da Vinci Code*.

An inductee of the Scottish Fashion Awards Hall of Fame and a recipient of the Royal Photographic Society's Centenary Medal, in 2007 a large-format print of a photograph he had taken in 1993 of the supermodel Kate Moss sold at auction for $108,000.

In the equally creative world of music, **Bruce Watson**, born in 1961 in Timmins, Ontario, is the Canadian-born Scottish guitarist who was a founder member, along with others who include the late Stuart Adamson, of the band Big Country.

Born in 1952 in Sheffield, **Christopher Watson** is a founder member of the experimental music groups Cabaret Voltaire and The Hafler Trio.

Now a sound recordist specialising in natural history, his 2003 album of 'field' recordings *The Weather Report*, has been named by the *Guardian* newspaper as "one of the thousand albums you should listen to before die."

The recipient of America's National Medal of Arts in 1997 and inducted into the North Carolina Music Hall of Fame two years before his death in 2012, Arthel Lane Watson was the blind musician better known as **Doc Watson**.

Born in 1923 in Deep Gap, North Carolina, he was also the recipient of seven Grammy Awards and a Grammy Lifetime Achievement Award in recognition of his pioneering contribution to the musical genres of folk, bluegrass, country, blues and gospel.

In a much different musical genre, **William Watson**, born in 1796 and who died in 1840, was the English concert hall singer and songwriter from Tyneside best known for his song *Dance To Thy Daddy*.

No account of the Watsons could perhaps be complete without a mention of a noted fictional character of the name – Dr Watson – who has achieved international fame as the trusty sidekick of the author Sir Arthur Conan Doyle's cerebral sleuth Sherlock Holmes, whose exploits were originally published in *The Strand Magazine* between 1891 and 1927.